GOOD GRIEF
for Broken Hearts

By

Crystal Jones

Good Grief for Broken Hearts

Copyright © 2021 by Crystal Jones

All Rights Reserved.

Edited, formatted, and published by

Destiny House Publishing, LLC.

P.O. Box 19774

Detroit, MI 48219

inquiry@destinyhousepublishing.com

www.destinyhousepublishing.com

404.993.0830

Cover by Kingdom Graphic Designs

This work may not be used in any form, or reproduced by any means, in whole or in part, without written permission from the publisher or author. Unless otherwise stated, all scripture is from the King James Version (KJV)

Printed in the United States

ISBN: 978-1-936867-74-5

Acknowledgments and Dedications

I would like to acknowledge my **Kind King** for his healing power. Lord, my healing is not complete just yet, but I thank you for walking me through the difficult seasons of my life. I am eternally grateful for the awesome privilege of intimate fellowship with You.

It is an incredible blessing that with all my own cracks and chips, You still see fit to use me to help others. I appreciate you. Thank you, Jesus, for all that you are, do, and speak. I love you.

I also would like to acknowledge my covenant partner for life, my husband and best friend, **Oscar Jones.** Babe, you are always so sensitive to me. Some seasons have been especially difficult, but you have always been there to hold me and speak God's word to me. Your words wash and uplift my heart. Thank you for being so strong in Christ, that you call forth strength in me. Thank you, my forever love.

I dedicate this book to all those who have suffered any type of loss. Hold on to the Lord and receive His love. He is able to navigate you through the pain. His promises are sure and His grace is magnificent.

Table of Contents

Acknowledgments and Dedications iii

Chapter 1: Getting to the Good Part 7

Chapter 2: What's So Good About Grief? 14

Chapter 3: How Do We Grieve? 20

Chapter 4: Sudden Death 32

Chapter 5: Cumulative Grief - Multiple Losses 41

Chapter 6: Unrealistic Expectations 48

Chapter 7: Why? 54

Chapter 8: Pure Grief 61

Chapter 9: Time's Up 68

Chapter 10: Strong People Cry 75

Chapter 11: Death Trap 82

Chapter 12: What Becomes of the Broken Hearted? 90

Scriptures for Comfort 98

About the Author 100

Chapter 1
Getting to the Good Part

I started grieving for my mother, years before she died. She displayed signs of dementia, probably 5 or 6 years before her death. At least, that's when I started noticing them. There was a definite shift in her persona. She wasn't the same bubbly, spicy woman that I had always known. She couldn't remember events and people. She was sad and broken. So by the time she went into hospice, I think I was nearing the end of my first grief of the loss of my mother as I had known her. She was <u>*mentally*</u> gone from me and <u>*emotionally*</u> she was slipping away. When she died this past January, that grief morphed into a new grief -the woman I loved was <u>*physically*</u> gone. I broke again. I had not previously understood that grief could have layers.

Grief does come in layers. And you break more than once. There are so many parts of your loved one's life to grieve. I was grieving my mom's role that was absent in my life. She could no longer "mother" me. My sister and I became her caretakers. I mourned the loss of her memory and my family history, as she couldn't recall vital information that I needed from her. I also grieved being able to have a simple conversation with her because many days she would sit in silence. I grieved being able to give her gifts that she could enjoy. I am a giver and wanted so much to lavish her with her heart's desires. You, too, will find yourself uncovering the layers.

Those who must deal with a family member diagnosed with dementia or Alzheimer's or some form of these diseases understand this precarious situation. The personality of your loved one is altered. Their memory and functionality shifts. Many times, the child becomes the caretaker. And the parent reverts back to their childhood days. They may or may not remember you. Sometimes they may think that you are a different family member or a perfect stranger. They tend to repeat stories over and over again. And they have a difficult time processing all that is going on around them, but they are keenly aware that something is not quite right within. Some lash out in anger, spewing venom at all in their circle. They cannot control their emotions.

It feels like your loved one has a slow leak in their soul. You lose a little part of them every day until the dementia (or other disease} completely takes over. Yes, loss is complex. And we have to understand that there are multiple aspects to our grief journey.

And there will be personal layers – specific to you. I had to grieve that my mother would never come home again. Later in her illness, she relocated from Michigan to California to be with my sister. I flew to see her every other month. She continued to say she didn't want to come back to Detroit, every time I asked her. I wanted her close. Eventually, she was too ill to transport.

It's been eight months since her transition from this life and my heart is still aching.

In the midst of such a devastating loss, I also lost my very closest friend. She was the godmother to my children, the one with whom I talked through these types of situations. She died from Covid-19 less than 4 months after my mother's death. It has been a lot to process. I miss her immensely.

I found myself in this gut-wrenching angst that I had not known before. I have experienced many losses over the years, but never grief this intense. I wrote this book to deal with my own grief and to help others to navigate their grief journey.

Grief is not as simple as we wish it were. It is not made to be stuffed but must be released. Grief encompasses the good, the bad and the ugly. We must experience the bad and the ugly in order to get to the good.

Death and loss are as much a part of life as love is. Love is enjoyable. Death and loss are not. Yet the pain we feel from death and loss are directly correlated to our love. Whether the love lost is an animal or a human, it demands a response. How we navigate grief is our response.

When we love, and that love is lost, we will feel the heartache. One famous quote goes, "Grief is the price we pay for love." Another quote, "Love comes before grief and love will be there, after." It's true, we don't stop loving because our family, friends or pets have gone on. We continue in love. And so we have to learn how to live after our loves are gone.

John 10:10 TPT reads, A thief has only one thing in mind—he

wants to steal, slaughter, and destroy. But I have come to *give you everything in abundance, more than you expect*—life in its fullness until you overflow!

I think that is an important scripture for this book. We need to keep the right perspective. The thief is the enemy. God is not a murderer or destroyer. Death and loss are in the world because of sin and Satan. But Jesus, Our Life Giver came to offer us something far better – life in abundance. It's a life brimming with love, hope, promises and blessings. In the midst of all the gloom and doom in this world, Jesus is the Light. And He has an amazing plan for each of us. That doesn't mean we will experience only good in this world. On the contrary, a world that is soaked in sin is destined to bring us loss and pain. The bright side is that we don't have to go though it alone. Our Faithful God promises to be right in there with us, holding our hands and loving us through it.

Maybe you are dealing with an illness, or some loved one has gotten a difficult diagnosis and you're afraid of what may be ahead. You could be dealing with the painful wounds of a close relationship. Or maybe you are having difficulty with death.

You've experienced loss before, but now the familiar has broken you in a way that you never imagined. I am glad that you made your way to this book. I have prayed for all those whose eyes would touch this book.

First, I want to say that I am sorry for the pain that you are in currently or will eventually go through. I understand that your heart is broken, even if no one else acknowledges it. It's a hard place. Death hurts. And often the ache suffers long.

I have prayed that our Loving Lord would comfort you and give you peace as you maneuver through this season of your life. God's desire is that you will have good grief. He extends an invitation to you to get to a heathy emotional life and new transitions. It requires only a willing heart. Good Grief is possible and necessary to get to wholeness when our hearts have been broken into a million pieces.

I want you to find a place where you can get alone with the Lord. This is your private time to grieve. Tune out all distractions. Take your time reading through each chapter. Underline, circle, dogear pages, highlight whatever stands out. This book is for you. Don't be afraid to write in it. Pause where you must. But take it all in. It's your invitation to good grief.

There is a section with questions at the end of each chapter called Getting to the Good Part. Answer each question honestly. Remember this book is for your eyes only. You can be transparent with yourself and with the Lord. Say what you wouldn't dare say in front of others because they may not understand. God does. I pray that you will get to the other side of your pain.

And we know that the only way to get over the pain is to go through it. I've prayed that you will go through it. Hold fast to your faith.

For his anger endureth but a moment; in his favour is life: weeping may endure for a night, but joy cometh in the morning. Psalm 30:5 KJV

Chapter 2
What's So Good About Grief?

Every good gift and every perfect gift is from above, and cometh down from the Father of lights, with whom is no variableness, neither shadow of turning. (James 1:17 KJV)

Grief is a beautiful gift from God. I know we don't think of it that way. I didn't. But the more I study grief, the more I understand it. It is one of those undervalued blessings that most of us don't normally appreciate until later in life. But grief is for our good.

It's God's offering to humans and animals to process loss. (Yes, animals grieve, too). Our Creator designed our bodies with natural channels for releasing the deep sadness we experience. Tears are one of those channels. They pour from our eyes and wash our hearts. Have you ever heard the expression, 'Having a good cry'? It's that feeling after you have cried your eyes out and it's all done. You feel good for having gone through it. Well that is how good grief works. It's a refreshing of our soul after a major emotional upheaval.

Grief is the processing of loss and death. It is a journey that none want to venture through. But we will all find it necessary when someone we love transitions into the next realm. There is no way around it. It's the proper way to adjust to loss. Our emotions have to adapt to the new vacancy.

Our loved one who was once on earth, filling up our lives, has moved from this earth, permanently. As a result, of their absence, our body responds: our heart hurts, the tears gush, and our head and stomach may ache. It seems our gait has slowed. And we grasp for understanding and peace.

Grief is the path that we must take, not just for death, but for any loss. Whether that loss is sickness, divorce, unemployment, incarceration, broken friendship, or miscarriage, etc. Loss leaves a gaping hole in our hearts that changes us forever. And so we must grieve. We must allow ourselves to feel the ache of what no longer remains. It is unhealthy to pretend that the pain isn't there or try to force ourselves past it.

Grief is the gift that God has afforded us to maneuver through losses and death. We have to make the trek to adjust to the life that has just hit us with a traumatic blow. When death or loss occur, our lives shift. And though we long for normal and the past, they will escape us. They are no longer possible.

We will grieve because we have been ejected into a life transition that we didn't want - nor were ready for. Everything in us screams for yesterday. We want everything to be put back in place. Unfortunately, it won't be. And that's what good grief is about. It's getting to that place where we can completely accept the death or loss and move forward in it.

We have to learn how to live differently. At the moment of the loss, we don't know how to do it. Good grief helps us to get on the other side of the pain. We get to breathe again and continue on with life. We adapt to the shift in our life. We create new patterns and routines.

We can function properly without being on autopilot, still enjoying and embracing life and all that it has to offer.

We grieve because we will miss the ones we loved so deeply (whether the relationships were good or bad). Some mistakenly think that just because the relationship was estranged that there is no grieving to be done. God covered all bases. We will still grieve those we had issues with.

Good Grief teaches us to cherish the past and look towards the future with new hope and expectation. We do remember those who have transitioned this life. We cherish our memories. Eventually our memories will make us laugh, smile, and exhale.

We learn gratitude through properly processing loss. We can thank God for the people and opportunities that have come into our lives. We had the immense privilege of loving some amazing people and being in relationship with them. We can be grateful for the time that we had, even though it was shorter than we would have chosen.

Grief also gives us a new perspective to handle what is remaining with compassion. Our emotions leave us raw and tender. We can extend to others what we have experienced ourselves.

Good grief also teaches us to avoid entitlement and assumption.

We may start out with a bad attitude, but we don't end there. We understand that we are not the only people in the world grieving. There are countless others. We don't demand anything from God because he has given us so much. Good grief reminds us that our blessings on this earth are temporal. Here today. Gone tomorrow.

We learn how to relish in the relationships that are remaining. We come out more mature on the other end. We love better, hug more, and forgive quicker.

The sunlight that breaks through the clouds after a torrential storm, that's what good grief does. It gradually leads you to the sunshine and helps you to heal again.

If you allow it, good grief will bring you closer to God. So welcome it. Embrace it. Let it come. Healthy grieving or, *good grief* will lead you to peace.

Getting to the Good Part:

1. Explain your current loss. It is important to be able to articulate what hurts.
2. When did your loss occur?

3. What have you learned so far from your grief?

4. What have you learned about yourself?

Chapter 3
How Do We Grieve?

"My life's strength melts away with grief and sadness; come strengthen me and encourage me with your words."
(Psalm 119:28 TPT)

Good Grief is unfamiliar to most of us. The average person often feels that they don't know how to grieve properly. We've been given mixed messages over the years. Some say just go with whatever you feel. Let the pain take you wherever it wants. Others say man up or woman up. They encourage you to stuff your emotions and be strong for others. So which is it?

If we are honest, we would have to admit that most of us have an aversion to grief. We want to stuff our emotions. We want to busy ourselves with work, ministry, and life to avoid the excruciating pain of loss. We would prefer to distract ourselves from feeling, even though we know it not to be appropriate.

Stuffing emotions is never good for any of us. And going with whatever you feel can be dangerous. Emotions are indicators. They help us to know where we are and what's going on with us. However we should not let our emotions be dictators of our behavior.

So what do you do with all the negative emotions that accompany loss?

Grief is too strong of an emotion to be suppressed or ignored. It demands to be felt. It will surface despite your greatest attempts at containing it.

As much as we want to avoid grief, fortunately, we don't get the option to escape it or shorten its grip. Grief will wait us out. It could take years, but grief will bubble up on the inside of us, sizzling for its release. Then it explodes, and we wonder, "Where did that come from?"

On the flip side, there are others who want the pain to remain forever. They feel like they don't deserve to be without the pain. The pain is all they have left of their loved one. And they are afraid to lose it. They want to wallow in it. In their eyes, letting go of the pain means that their loved one will be forgotten, and memories erased. Of course, this is not true. They will have to navigate their way to that understanding. It's really ok to move forward. Actually, it's necessary.

While the expression of grief is different for every person, there are still healthy ways to grieve.

Grieving has frequent ebbs and flows. You will have both good days and bad. You can go several consecutive days doing just fine and then the next day can send you into a tailspin of tears. You may feel stuck or like you are suffocating or aching in sadness. One grief-stricken friend put it; "I feel like I'm swimming in mud".

Loss can be experienced as any of the listed physical attributes:

- Feelings of heaviness in the chest or a tightness in the throat.
- A loss of appetite

- An empty feeling in the stomach
- Overwhelming feeling of disbelief, fear, or anxiety
- Crying, restlessness
- Memory gaps, difficulty concentrating or focusing.
- Headaches and stomachaches
- Dreaming the deceased is alive
- Oversleeping and insomnia

When the person you love dies, your mind can play tricks on you. You can sometimes forget that the deceased isn't in this earthly realm, any longer. You may pick up the phone expecting to call them and remember at that moment, that they are gone. Maybe you dream that they aren't really dead. It was all a mistake. Or you think you see them in public. You may even drive to their house before it hits you, that your loved one is gone. It happens. It's a type of wrangling the deceased from your present and placing them into your past. Your mind knows but your heart isn't quite ready for it. And so it hurts...deeply.

These are typical responses to loss. But everyone has his/her own physical response pattern. Some people may experience all of these or even none of these.

Then there are what psychologists call the stages of loss. Some say there are anywhere from 5 to 12. However the 5 stages tend to be the standard. So I have listed them for you. These are not chronological steps. Because grief is very personal and complex, there is really no particular order to the stages.

The 5 stages of loss are:

- **Denial:** You may feel shocked or numb. This is a defense mechanism. It's hard to believe or process that the loss has occurred.

- **Anger:** Frustration and helplessness can lead you to anger. It can be directed at nearly anyone, including yourself or the deceased.

- **Bargaining:** This is the state of going back and forth about what could have happened differently. Common thoughts are "If only…" "What if…" You may also try to strike a deal with God.

- **Depression:** This is the state of sadness or heavy feeling that is experienced in loss. This is not deep depression or clinical depression that doesn't allow you to function.

- **Acceptance:** This is the place where you can accept the reality of the death or loss. You may feel twinges of sadness, but you are able to move forward and enjoy life again.

These stages are the way we emotionally experience the process. And there is nothing that says you must enter all 5 stages.

Generally we don't feel the same level of grief for each loss we experience. For some, its deeper and more intense. There are so many variables. It just depends on our relationship with the deceased, our own season of life, and our perspective on death.

In my years of dealing with my own grief and the grief of others, I have learned a lot of interesting things about grief. There are at least 16 types of grief: Abbreviated, Absent, Anticipatory, Chronic, Collective, Complicated, Cumulative, Delayed, Disenfranchised, Distorted, Exaggerated, Inhibited, Masked, Prolonged, Traumatic and Normal Grief (which is what I call Good Grief).

When you are studying grief, the task itself can be

overwhelming. There is so much information to digest.

We won't cover all of the types of grief in this book. But I will talk about a few of them.

How does one actually grieve in a healthy way? First and foremost, you don't avoid it. If you feel like crying, you let the tears fall. If you want to look at old pictures, you pull out your album. If you want to remember a story or share a memory, you contact someone who will listen.

Don't act as if the loss has not occurred. Don't pretend that you are immune to the pain or try to act super spiritual. Feel the pain. Talk to God about what you feel. Trust Him to bring you through it. Good Grief is letting go of the pain in slow motion.

We also have to be careful about comparing sorrows. When we do not process our grief properly, we can find ourselves looking at others with envy. It is the anger side of grief. You may wonder, "Why does that person still have their child, spouse, or parent? Why couldn't I have mine? Is God against me? Does God love me less?"

Laurie's 25-year-old daughter, Kayleigh had recently received a doctor's report that she would need to have a mastectomy of her right breast. Laurie was struggling with so much anger. She continually compared her life to others, feeling dejected by God. When she spoke with a nurse at the hospital, she discovered that the nurse's daughter had the same diagnosis but had been supernaturally healed in a church service. Laurie thought, "How unfair! Why doesn't God supernaturally heal my daughter?" Laurie felt herself being angry at God and jealous of the nurse. She said to the nurse, "At least you don't have to go through this with your daughter." The nurse looked at her and said, "Yes, I thank God for His goodness." As she continued to talk to the nurse, she discovered that the nurse had lost her husband and her grandson in a tragic car accident a little over a year ago. Guilt poured over Laurie.

Comparing sorrows is a tool of the enemy. It is unproductive and unkind. You don't want to wish bad on someone else. Every person has their own cross to bear. One person may have a loss in one area, and someone else - in another. But we all need to lean on the Lord and hope in Him.

We can trust Him with our deepest hurts. He is near to those who are crushed. Tell him what you cannot tell others. He wants to hear your voice. In those times, where you cannot speak, he will hear your heart.

Grieving well requires that we intentionally act. We can't just float through our grief with our emotions as our guide.

Experiencing loss makes us sensitive and vulnerable. You will feel a range of emotions. And it's important to examine them. But we can't just go with what we feel. You may feel angry and want to harm someone. You shouldn't allow that emotion to dictate your actions. It is more beneficial to explore why you are so angry. Journaling about your anger will yield better results.

Prayer is essential during this season. Talk to God even if you have been distant in your relationship with Him. He is always ready to talk to you. Don't let guilt keep you from Him.

Establishing a daily routine of prayer may help you feel a sense of security. It doesn't have to be a long prayer, but a time to acknowledge God and ask for his help.

Meditation on scripture can soothe the heart. There are some scriptures at the back of this book to help.

Set a time to wake up and go to sleep every day. Avoid caffeine to prevent insomnia. It is also not a good idea to try to sleep through the pain. Keep your sleep regulated. Don't allow your days to meld into one another.

Some people attempt to deal with the pain with drugs and alcohol. This only makes things worse. Extend good care to yourself. You are the one that God has assigned this important task. Make sure you are getting enough sleep, eating healthy foods, drinking lots of water, and doing some type of exercise.

Taking good care of yourself will help you feel better. Involve yourself in activities that help you to have peace. That could be cooking, painting, writing, meditation, golf, crochet. Whatever activity feeds your soul. Do what you need to do to be healthy, even if you have to push yourself to do it.

You may also find personal counseling to provide solace. It is good to talk out your pain. A grief counselor, pastor, or friend can help you navigate your emotions.

Joining a support group can also prove to be beneficial.

Proverbs 11:14 says, Where there is no [wise, intelligent] guidance, the people fall [and go off course like a ship without a helm], But in the abundance of [wise and godly] counselors there is victory.

It's a good idea to have at least one person that you can lean on during this season.

Extend patience and grace to yourself. Experiencing loss is intense and messy. None of us do it perfectly. You will have days that you feel like you are strong. But there will be "weak days" as well. In those times, you may feel like your whole world is falling apart. Just know that His strength is made perfect in your weakness. God has enough grace for those times. He will undergird you and help you through it.

The Lord is the Good Shepherd, our Daddy God. His love for you never fails and is not based on your actions. Lean into His love. Bask in it. Draw comfort and peace from Him and know that He cares.

Getting to the Good Part:

1. What type of grief are you experiencing?
2. Are you stuffing your grief?
3. What stage of grief are you in?

4. What are some activities that you have already put in place to help you grieve properly?

5. Identify one person that you can talk to during this season.

6. Reach out to her/him.

Chapter 4
Sudden Death

Even though I walk through the [sunless] valley of the shadow of death, I will fear no evil, for You are with me; Your rod [to protect] and Your staff [to guide], they comfort and console me. (Psalms 23:4 AMP)

The shock of a loss is especially challenging to navigate when it occurs unexpectantly and abruptly; murder, suicide, Covid-19, fire, a car accident, heart attack, stroke, drowning, sudden onset of illness, etc. Grieving through a shock is called traumatic grief.

While the pain of grief is the same whether the loss is sudden or anticipated, a sudden or traumatic loss is jolting and can leave you feeling off-balanced and disoriented.

Expected death allows you time to brace for what's coming. But sudden death does not. It can leave you off-balanced and render you paralyzed. It's abrupt and offensive.

Traumatic grief feels surreal and can leave you staggering in a state of disbelief. You are left with unfinished business, unspoken sentiment, and missed opportunities. It can cause you to feel disconnected from friends, family members and even God. You try to figure out what happened and what it means. You find yourself in a continual state of dizziness with a myriad of questions. It is hard to process because you don't have a sense of closure. This can certainly affect your ability to cope.

Not every sudden or catastrophic loss results in traumatic grief. Some people can process through it without complicated bereavement. But others may show signs of both trauma and grief. They go from one extreme to the other. They might avoid talking about the person they lost altogether, or they might become fixated on the way their loved one died.

Our heart says that our loved one should not have died. It doesn't make sense to us. So we begin to assign blame. We can blame doctors, other health care workers, places of employment, hospitals, family members, etc. You may even blame your loved one. They should not have gone to a certain place, or they should have taken better care of themselves. This is a natural thought process when unexpected death occurs.

Sometimes the blame turns inward and is manifested as guilt. You can find yourself second-guessing even the smallest detail. Should I have done something different? Maybe if I would have chosen a different hospital or a different doctor or hid my prescription from them?

These thoughts of guilt come straight from the enemy of our souls. He wants to torment us. And the more we meditate on what we could have done differently, the more the enemy is able to condemn us and keep us locked in the spirit of self-degradation.

Romans 8:1 reads, there is therefore now no condemnation to those who are in Christ Jesus who walk not after the flesh but after the Spirit.

Unfortunately, when we focus on the 'how', that can consume us. There are so many what-if scenarios that can try to suck you in like quicksand. It is futile. Trying to figure out what you could have done differently is not going to bring your loved one back. Nor will it help you to heal. It is unhealthy to become obsessed with how a person exited this earth. The mental torment can be exhausting. No matter how a person died, the hurt will still be present. Worrying about the method only adds insult to injury. We can't choose how any of us will leave this world. We just know that we will.

Our Loving Lord sits at the right hand of the Father making intercession for us. God does not want you stuck in this unfruitful cycle. He wants you to have peace.

Process the 'how' of your loss, but don't stay there. There are some questions you will never get the answers to. The how can anchor you to the pain. If you feel that you can't get past it, then it may be an indicator that you should talk to a professional to help you get through it.

Traumatic loss is multidimensional. You may have had your own ideas and plans for your decedent that will not be realized. You expected your loved one's life to be something different. Maybe they recently purchased a new house or car; or booked a cruise that they won't get to experience. Perhaps your loved one was just starting a new job, had a new baby or recently married. We are broken hearted because of a life that our loved one didn't get to live. All of the plans and ideas that they had or we had for them are left undone. That's another one of those layers we have to grieve. We grieve their hopes and dreams unrealized. Maybe the deceased hoped to marry or have a baby - but didn't. It's like putting together a puzzle with missing pieces. You will grieve what you thought their story should have been.

Generally, those who deal with traumatic loss also struggle with anger. But anger won't correct the loss. You will need to admit it. Determine who you are angry with and why. Sometimes anger is appropriate. But you can't hold on to it. Do the work to get through it. That's not easy, but it is necessary. Once you let go of the anger you can get on with mourning the loss of your loved one.

That doesn't mean you won't mourn both parts at the same time. You may. Remember when it comes to grief, it's very personal.

Let me add, God is not a murderer. He is a life-giving God.

When he grants each of us breath, it's a timed breath. We will wake up only so many days. And then it will all be over. Regardless of *how* we check out, we will check out. Hebrews 9:27 AMP says, "And just as it is appointed and destined for all men to die once and after this [comes certain] judgment."

The time is past, and our loved ones are gone. Death snuck up on us when we weren't expecting it. How do we process it?

We can't go back and undo things or unsay what was said. We can't acquire for them things that they weren't meant to have. Their chapter on earth is closed…forever. Their mission is complete.

Jesus didn't die of a ripe old age. He transitioned this life at the tender age of 33. He was beaten and maliciously murdered. Yet, his death wasn't premature. He died when he was supposed to die. Even though the circumstances of his death seemed to suggest he died prematurely. He didn't. He laid down his life at the precise moment appointed. He had finished his assignment. Of course, the good news is that Jesus didn't stay dead.

And our loved ones who die in Christ, won't stay dead either.

When our friends/family die in the Lord, they have a promise from God for something far greater. II Corinthians 5:8 we are [as I was saying] of good courage and confident hope and prefer rather to be absent from the body and to be at home with the Lord.

Traumatic grief can take you places you really do not want to go.

The best thing we can do is grieve well and make peace with the Lord. We didn't know our loved one was going to leave the earth so soon, but God did. He could have let us know it would happen, but he didn't. Or maybe He did, but we didn't recognize the signs. He could have extended their time on the earth, but he, in his infinite wisdom, didn't feel that was appropriate. Isaiah 55:8-9 AMP reads, "For My thoughts are not your thoughts, Nor are your ways My ways," declares the LORD. "For as the heavens are higher than the earth, so are my ways higher than your ways and My thoughts higher than your thoughts."

There is a lot we won't understand on this side. That's where trust comes in.

Whatever joy you wanted for your loved one on earth, they have exceeded that in eternity. Psalm 16:11 reads, "You will show me the path *of* life; In Your presence is *fullness of joy*; In Your right hand there are pleasures forevermore." Their joy is complete. It is at its maximum capacity. Our loved ones who die in the Lord, given the opportunity, would not come back to the earth for any reason. You would not be able to persuade them to leave out of the anointed presence of the Holy Lord to come back to this sin cursed earth. Just as you may wish they were here, imagine them wishing you were there. It's just better on the other side.

If you find yourself in a long-term struggle with the timing of your loved one's transition or the way they transitioned, give yourself some grace. Trauma makes grief a little tougher. And it can take a little longer to work through. In the meantime, talk to God about it. Journal. And seek out professional help if you need to.

Getting to the Good Part:

1. Are you dealing with a traumatic loss?
2. What was the trauma? And how are your processing it?

3. What do you wish you had done or said to the decedent?

4. Do you blame yourself in any way? Or God?

5. Have you found yourself comparing losses?

Chapter 5
Cumulative Grief - Multiple Losses

He heals the brokenhearted and binds up their wounds [healing their pain and comforting their sorrow] (Psalm 147:3 AMP)

A strong wind blew the house down. Unfortunately, all 10 of the couple's children were in the house when it collapsed, and they all died – 7 boys and 3 girls. That's devastating! That was bad enough, but the loss of their 10 children wasn't their only loss.

Before that happened, there were several other losses. The worst part of it was that all of these losses occurred in the same day. The scriptures said while one servant was speaking telling Job about one trauma, another servant showed up to tell him something else, again and again. His servants were killed, his flocks were destroyed, and his camels were stolen. Add to that, he also was very ill.

Job had both traumatic and cumulative grief to navigate. Can you imagine? That had to be the worst season of his life. Have you ever had a season like that? It can feel like there is a storm cloud over your house, but the sun is shining on everyone else.

Loss piled on top of loss can be overwhelming and can make you feel like you can't breathe. It's crushing. It's a rough season to maneuver.

Epidemics and pandemics like the Covid-19 disease have ravaged families. Mass shootings, hurricanes, tsunamis, floods, plane, and car crashes can result in multiple losses.

But it's not always some catastrophic event, sometimes losing several family members from different causes over a specified period of time is the cumulative loss that takes its toll on families.

My husband and I have had a few seasons like that. One season was in 2003. Currently, I am in another season of cumulative loss, even as I write this. It's the heaviest I've ever experienced in my 59 years on the earth. My mom, grandmother, stepdad, godmother, my closest friend, an aunt, and about 5 other loved ones have died in the past two years. Eleven losses in 2 years and I suspect that I am not at the end of it. Cumulative losses are hard on the heart.

So how do you process grief overload? How do you get over one when there are fresh wounds to tend to? I've been asked this question multiple times.

The simple answer is you go through them clinging tightly to the Lord. The more complex answer is that you must deal with every loss both individually and wholistically.

I'm sure Job grieved the loss of his 10 children wholistically, but I'm sure he also grieved them separately. You have a unique relationship with each person who died, so you can't expect because you grieved one person that you don't have to grieve another. Sometimes the losses are so frequent that it's hard to know which loss you are grieving.

It is distressing to have to endure multiple losses. You can become vulnerable to self-pity. The enemy tries to convince you that God doesn't care or that he has abandoned you or that you have gotten on his bad side.

God reminds us in His word, I will never leave nor forsake you. I am with you to the ends of the earth. Marinate on that promise. God is with you even when you don't feel him. When you feel He is far away, He is there. That's a huge comfort - God is with you. If you are going through a "Job" season, know that God is in it with you. He is watching over you to perform his word. It doesn't mean that you did something wrong to bring this season upon yourself. You are not being reprimanded. God doesn't punish us by killing someone else.

Job was upright. He did not err. Actually, it was Job's steadfast devotion to God, that attracted the enemy's attack. It was Satan that attacked Job. Not God.

People have the tendency to blame God when bad things happen. But not Job. After Job received all the bad news of his compounded losses, the scripture says, Job worshipped.

[20] Then Job arose, and rent his mantle, and shaved his head, and fell down upon the ground, and worshipped,

[21] And said, Naked came I out of my mother's womb, and naked shall I return thither: the LORD gave, and the LORD hath taken

away; blessed be the name of the LORD.

²² In all this Job sinned not, nor charged God foolishly.

In the midst of his grief, he held on to God. That's how we get through cumulative losses, we worship God. We give praise to God's Holy name and honor to His character. We bless Him because He is good and there is no evil in Him. He is never plotting against us. We have to understand it's a season that we will get through. This too shall pass.

When we have a lot of people we love, there are a lot of people to lose. We all will experience sorrow in this life because there is a real devil and sin is in the earth. No other reason.

Some may say, "I don't think I can take much more. It's too much." Whenever we feel crushed, we can trust that God is always there to help us through it. The Lord never stepped away from Job and He won't step away from you, either. The scripture says that He is near to the brokenhearted.

Some just want to bury their heads and hearts in avoidance. Avoidance is no cure for grief; it only postpones it to a later time. Avoiding grief will cause cumulative grief to explode. In fact, a new loss can open up the wound to a previous one or a forgotten loss.

God is smart. He has intricately designed our emotions to deal with left over loss. If a person has not properly grieved their deceased or avoided some loss, that grief will show up in a dream, vision, or memory. We don't get to skip it.

Multiple losses can make you feel that everything is unsettled and there is nothing stable or certain in life. The sensation of it all can throw you off base and question your relationship with God.

Practically how do we deal with multiple losses?

- It's a good time to push the pause button. Take time to catch your breath and process. If that means taking time to get away for a day or weekend, do it. You can't stop the losses from coming, but you can retreat for strength and healing.

- Talk to someone: A friend, family member, pastor. Let someone else in.

- Be transparent with the Lord about how you feel. He knows. And can help you make sense of some things to get your bearings back.

God is certain when nothing else is. He is our Rock, steadfast and sure. There is no shadow of turning in Him. He is the same yesterday, today, and tomorrow. We can rest in that stability. We can lean on His faithfulness. He promises to bring us through tough times. Hopefully we come out of this season a whole lot closer to God.

Getting to the Good Part:

1. Have you ever experienced a Job season or are you in one now?

2. If so, what are the parts to your compound losses?

3. Have you been able to process them properly?

4. How are you handling your grief?

5. How is your relationship with God?

Chapter 6
Unrealistic Expectations

And be ye kind one to another, tenderhearted, forgiving one another, even as God for Christ's sake hath forgiven you. (Ephesians 4:32 KJV)

There may be times that while we are grieving the loss of the one who transitioned this life, we are also dealing with the hurt of those who we feel weren't there for us.

Maybe your loved one had a long sickness, and you were left to tend to them alone. Those who were supposed to help – didn't. Or maybe the bulk of the responsibility fell on you. There may be those who mistreated your loved one or were distant and cold towards them. Instead of rallying in support, they backed up or totally abandoned the deceased. Or perhaps it was at their death that close friends and family disappeared. You may have felt alone and abandoned.

The hurt is real. The one is connected to the other. We hurt because we felt those who were absent should not have been. While your pain is genuine, you will have to work towards forgiving all involved or not involved. In order to do that, we need to understand that expecting others to process loss in the same way we do, is unfair. The person may have had a difficult or strained relationship with the deceased and have their own journeys to take. Unrealistic expectations will always result in disappointment.

Everyone doesn't process sickness and death in the same way. Some people are so consumed with fear of loss or death that they are unable to even attend their loved one's funeral. Some are still living with unprocessed hurt, which can cause inertia. We all have issues in one area or another. It doesn't make those who are offended, bad people. They are unhealed people. It is unreasonable to expect people to act like we do.

At any rate, there is a gaping wound that is left to tend to. Often, we are so distracted by the death, that we don't deal with it. We feel it and know that it's there, but we leave it for the time being, hoping to either confront the offender later or withdraw from them completely.

When the dust has settled, we may find ourselves nursing the wound and refusing to let it go. We want the offender to see the scar left behind. Because our loved one is no longer here and what has been done cannot be fixed or undone. In our minds the behavior of the offender makes the pain feel more intense.

It is necessary that we separate the loss of the loved one from the behavior of the offender. These are two separate issues and must be dealt with as such. If we are going to get to good grief, it requires that we forgive. The word of God is still applicable. We are to forgive those who have offended us **and** those who have offended our loved ones.

We don't get to carry the pain and offer it as guilt to others. If we are going to grieve well, we have to choose forgiveness. It's the only way to start the healing process.

Michelle had a very close and intimate relationship with her biological father. Her parents had been divorced and both had remarried. Michelle was the eldest of the 3 adult children. Her dad was an alcoholic for most of their lives. He was sober the last 5 years. Michelle and her dad had worked out their issues years prior. But her other siblings had not. Her brother and sister were both very angry at their father. Michelle was hurt that her brother and sister were not there for their dad as he lay dying of cancer. They didn't want anything to do with him. They only visited him once before he died. And neither of them helped Michelle plan his funeral. After everything was over, Michelle was left with her heart stinging from the offenses of her siblings because they were not there for her or for her dad.

She held on to so much anger at their responses that she stopped speaking to both of them. She was transferring her dad's pain to herself. Or at least what she imagined his pain to be. That's not good grief.

Michelle needed to learn to let go of her unrealistic expectations. Her siblings would have to navigate their own paths in life. It doesn't make sense to expect their behavior to change because her father was sick or even that he died. Their pain doesn't dissipate. It's still there. Neither should she take it personally. His relationship with her siblings had nothing to do with her. Her siblings' relationship was between them and their dad.

It was easy for her to excuse her dad's past behavior. She had already processed her pain. Their pain was still unprocessed. It was unfair for her to expect them to act in a way that they had not healed to.

We all have to get to good grief from wherever we are. Being angry at her siblings was not going to produce the result that Michelle wanted. It only served to make her feel worse. And provoke more offense from her siblings. In fact, she was now demonstrating behavior that she was accusing her siblings of – unforgiveness.

We have to make peace with the fact, that everyone is flawed. Loved ones may struggle with offering you the emotional support that you need. It could be because they have wounds from the deceased. Or maybe the person is struggling with their own grief of a previous death. Sometimes one completely unrelated death can be a trigger for another. The stoic, unsupportive, family member or friend could be unaware - until one day they collapse in grief.

Whatever the case, do not allow the deceased's perceived pain to become yours. You have your own complex emotions to process. You don't need anything extra. Don't be quick to judge those who are struggling. Pray that they will forgive. Support and encourage them to do the work they will need to do to get to a good place.

At the end of the day, we simply need to live, love, and let live. That's what we are called to do. People have their own relationships to navigate. We can't do it for them. We can pray for them, offer support, and love them through it.

Getting to the Good Part:

1. Is there someone who wasn't there for you during your loss?
2. Is there someone who neglected or harmed your loved one preceding their death?
3. If so, how have you processed that hurt?
4. Journal to express your feelings about the offender and the forgiveness that needs to be rendered.

Chapter 7

Why?

O death, where is thy sting? O grave, where is thy victory?
(I Corinthians 15: 55 KJV)

Sometimes in the middle of grief we can think that the death of our loved one is something that God has done to us. It certainly feels like it. And it's hard to reconcile deep loss in our brains because our hearts feel like they have been ripped in two. And for what reason?

When my closest friend and the godmother of my children died, I wrestled. I talked to her the night before she went on the ventilator, not knowing that I would never be able to hear her voice again. We had been in relationship as friends for more than 44 years. We grew up together. Other than my husband, she knew me in a way that no one else did. I had prayed for her healing and speedy recovery. I had also enlisted the prayers of others. But she died. And I was devastated.

I remember she asked me, "Why did the Lord allow me to get Covid-19?" I didn't know. She had been careful. She wore her masks and stayed in. I didn't have the answers. But I was sure she would recover. She seemed to be responding well to the meds. She requested to go home. The doctors felt that was okay. But she quickly returned to the hospital, sicker than before. The next day, she was unresponsive. I had flown to the hospital to pray for her. Still no response. Nothing. My closest friend and confidant was gone.

My husband and I helped her only son to plan the service. And we were the officiates. We flew back home and just like that - it was all over. I felt like my heart had been ransacked.

And I found myself with the same questions that others are left to ponder, "Why? Why did my loved one have to die? Why didn't God heal her? Why?"

We can sometimes feel betrayed by God. Because He didn't do what we expected him to do. Did I have enough faith? Did I pray hard enough? What did I do wrong?

As we sort through our pain, we will have to understand that God didn't *do* this to us. Your loved one's death had nothing to do with you. He or she died because death is in this earth realm. Your loved one's healing was not dependent on how hard you prayed or how earnestly you sought the Lord. God was not punishing you. Hebrews 9:27 reads, And just as it is appointed *and* destined for all men to die once and after this [comes certain] judgment. It is expected that most of us will experience death.

Nevertheless, we can ask the questions. God is not an angry dictator, but a loving Father. He invites our conversations and intimate fellowship. Yet, He remains sovereign. He will determine the questions for which we are ready for the answers.

So let's explore this question of why.

The first couple of scripture has their story unveiled in the 2nd chapter of Genesis. Adam and Eve were created in God's image and enjoyed time in His presence. God loved on them and prepared them a paradise with everything they could imagine and then some. They encountered the slimy serpent who told them that God was evil, and they should not listen to him. He went on to say that God was holding out on them. He convinced them to eat the fruit that God told them not to eat, so that they would become like God. Forgetting that they were already like God, they ate the fruit. They trusted the one they didn't know who hadn't given them anything over the one they had a relationship with who had given them all things.

Consequently, sin entered the earth, bringing with it, suffering and death. As a result, we hurt and have pain. We get sick with diseases. We have accidents and trauma. We die. These are the repercussions of sin.

We will all have to meet Jesus either in the rapture or by the portal of death. Our assignment on earth is time stamped. We all have an expiration date that we are not privy to. Some die young and some die old. But we all will leave this sphere one way or another. It is simply the cycle of life. Every living thing will expire.

In our current culture, we tend to ascribe to the thought that if we are in God, we should not suffer. We can have everything we want and pray for. That line of reasoning cannot be found in scripture. Jesus encouraged us to take up our cross and follow Him. Some people were healed in scripture, and some were not. He brought some back from the dead, most were not. That is the sovereignty of God. We are too human to know what is best and what is not. Our understanding is limited by our humanity.

Obedience does yield blessing, but sometimes the blessing is also in the suffering. That's for our Omniscient God to determine.

The benefit of suffering is that it tends to draw us closer to God. Like a baby who reaches for his parents when in pain, so do we reach out for our Faithful Father in the midst of trouble. And our Loving Lord always reaches back to lift us up. He stands beside us in the toughest of times, wrapping his grace-filled arms around us. He is our comfort and strength. He never intends for us to suffer alone. He is there to calm us and pour out his love upon us.

We have to make peace with the fact that all life on the earth is temporary. Jesus didn't come in human form to stay. He was publicly murdered on a cross with government consent. Lies, jealousy, betrayal and hatred were the catalysts for his death. Sin. Yes, it was sin that hung him.

He was not guilty of any of the wrongdoing for which He was accused. Still He died. Jesus died for sin. He died to redeem us from it. Of course, the good news is Jesus was resurrected. He woke up from death to give us all hope and victory. Sin separated us from God, but Jesus overcame death and the grave. He died for mankind to be reconciled to the Father. Jesus now offers us a life hidden in him that will yield us the opportunity to live forever. Death does not have the final say. We will see our loved ones who die in Christ again on the other side.

There will be a new heaven and a new earth. There will be no more crying, no more death in the afterlife. Because sin will be no more.

Getting to the Good Part:

1. Write a description of life in essay form or poetry. Or paint a picture that represents life for you right now.
2. What is the promise of everlasting life?
3. What legacy has your loved one left behind?

4. What legacy do you want to leave?

Chapter 8
Pure Grief

"Let your light so shine before men, that they may see your good works, and glorify your Father which is in heaven."
(Matthew 5:16 KJV)

A mother and her adult daughter were arguing over an issue. The situation got heated and the more they argued, the worse it got. When they left each other's presence, they stopped speaking to each other. This was not unusual for their toxic relationship. They both were very stubborn. The mother was controlling. And the daughter was harsh. After a few weeks of their silent war, the mother died in her sleep.

Of course, this devastated the daughter. She was recked with guilt and anger. Before she could even get to her grief, she had to deal with the other emotions she was feeling. She tried to push through it. She was exasperated. The pain of her grief was severe.

When someone dies, there is sometimes unfinished business. Maybe we didn't get the opportunity to say, 'Good-bye' or 'I'm sorry' or 'I forgive you'. We didn't get to say all the things that we should have or take back some of the things that we did. We took life for granted because we thought we would have more time. But just like that mother and daughter, the clock can catch us off guard. This can leave us with so much left to process.

I was actually prepared for my mother's death when she took her last breath. Some people say you can't be prepared in death, but I believe that you can. That doesn't mean you won't feel the pain of it. Nor does it mean you won't have to grieve. In fact, I am still grieving her death. But being prepared for her death means that everything else was in order. Not just her final arrangements, but also in our relationship. There were no offenses between us. She and I talked about her relationship with the Lord. I talked to her about forgiving others and asked for forgiveness from her, if there were some things remaining. We had worked on our relationship during her season of illness, and we were loving on each other when she left me. The best memory I have is my mother telling me how much she loved me, nearly every time I talked to her. Even those days when she didn't feel like talking, she would blow me kisses. She never forgot my name or who I was to her (I asked the Lord for this gift). At the end of her life, I only had to deal with losing her physical presence. There was nothing else to grieve.

Pure grief is when we only have grief to process. We can get through it easier and faster. But if we have to process other negative emotions, things get a little stickier.

If your relationship with the deceased was difficult or damaged, this will certainly add another layer to your grief. It can take some extra time and thought before you are able to look back on the relationship and adjust to the loss. You may have to process hurt from the deceased or work through a cloud of other emotions before you can get to peace.

If your loss is muddied with regret, offense, bitterness, unforgiveness, shame, and guilt, grieving is different. All of these negative emotions hinder grief and can compound the pain. You must sift through the fog of issues that are present, in order to forgive, so that you can properly grieve.

We can't just go directly to pure grief from a toxic or dysfunctional relationship. We have to deal with any other unsettled emotions that exist. Otherwise you will find yourself unable to experience good grief. Anger will choke the love right out of you.

When a person is falling apart or just not handling grief properly, it is usually because they do not have pure grief. They have some other issues with the deceased that are unresolved. Or sometimes the issue is with themselves. They could be consumed with guilt. Maybe they could have done more or treated their loved one better.

So what do you do when you don't have pure grief?

Pray: ask God to help you identify and navigate the negative emotions present.

Write a letter to the Lord about your deceased loved one to clear the air. Include all of the things you should have said and talked about before their departure. This could take weeks to complete. You are not in a rush. Keep it in a safe place away from the eyes of others. This is a private matter, not to be shared with anyone else. When your emotions are in alignment and you feel a release in your spirit, then go ahead and burn or tear up the letter.

Forgive the deceased. It's not too late. As long as you have breath in your body, you have the ability to forgive.

Ask God to forgive you. He most certainly will. I John I:9 reads, If we confess our sins, he is faithful and just to forgive us our sins, and to cleanse us from all unrighteousness.

His love covers a multitude of sins.

Forgive yourself. For all have sinned and come short of the glory of God. Romans 3:23. We are all flawed. But that is no reason to continually beat yourself up. God cares about you.

If you are still suffering, you may need help to process the relationship. That could mean getting into counseling/therapy. A good therapist can help you unpack the relationship so that you can get to good grief. Pray when choosing a therapist or ask someone for a recommendation. All therapists and counselors are not the same. Some are healthier than others.

That's why it's important to ask God for direction.

Too often, we assume we have plenty of time to right the wrongs of relationships. But truth is we don't have a clue how much time is left for the other person or for ourselves. That is why it is best to live life by loving and forgiving. Don't keep excusing yourself from the real work of relationships. Forgive and ask for forgiveness.

Do what you can now, so that you won't have to live in regret later. That means we should be relationally ready to transition from this life at any moment. This requires that we:

- Be in right relationship with God
- Forgive quickly.
- Don't sweat the small stuff.
- Give people more than what they deserve.
- Trust God to avenge us.

In fact, this is what the Bible teaches us. We are to love people the way that God loves us. That's a big order. God is merciful, compassionate, and kind. He loves us whether we are good to Him or not.

So go love all the people in your life that are still here. Don't make the mistakes of leaving things undone. Let it be true that when your loved ones transition from this earth – that all you have is pure grief.

Getting to the Good Part:

1. Did you and your loved one have a good relationship?

2. Are you offended by your deceased loved one? If so, why?

3. Do you have any regrets?

4. Do you need to forgive them?

5. Write your letter to the Lord to deal with any residue from the death of your loved one.

Chapter 9
Time's Up

To every thing there is a season, and a time to every purpose under the heaven: ⁴A time to weep, and a time to laugh; a time to mourn, and a time to dance; (Ecclesiastes 3:1, 4 KJV)

How long is one expected to grieve? When will pain of loss and grief end?

We do not like to live with pain. But loss forces us into this area of discomfort.

There is good news. Because God has Lordship over grief, we can know that grief is only temporary. It will come to an end. The aches of our heart are not permanent. As we continue to move through the grieving process, the pain will lessen. The intensity of the pain usually fades with time. While we may still feel twinges from the loss, we do recover from the devastation of the trauma it caused.

However, sometimes our expectations are im- practical. I have talked to people who have said, "But it's been 3 months, 6 months, or a year. Shouldn't I be over this by now?" They believe their grief is no longer valid because they have assessed a time that it should be done.

The thing about grief is we don't get to determine when it's done. It doesn't come with a specific timetable. Often, we wish it did. We want to get on with it, so that we can be over it. But the reality is - grief takes however long it takes. And that's usually longer than we would like.

We judge ourselves too harshly when we set our clocks to our grief. We can feel ashamed that we still feel the pain. As a result, we try to hide our grief and pretend that we are good. That's certainly not healthy.

If your grief is still present after several months, or even a year, deal with it. It's just a signal that you may have more work to do in processing your loss.

Anything that reminds us of people or our pets who have died can trigger our pain by making us aware of the void. Holidays, birthdays, or other celebrations are the big triggers. Or it could be seeing their name or a photo that activates you.

For me, it was a Facebook memory. My mother had posted on my page that she was looking for me and she loved me several years ago. And it popped up recently as I was scrolling on the site. I cried.

Another day, it was the cream PT Cruiser parked on the street. My God-sister drove one just like it. Seeing that car made me remember her.

The truth is we will never forget those that we loved. And we will always miss their presence. That's a fact.

As long as we don't get stuck in the loss and can experience life's joys. That's okay.

If it has been 2 years or more, and your pain is still lingering, there is a chance that your grief might be prolonged or complicated. Prolonged or complicated grief speaks to the way that we experience the loss. This type of grief can take you into clinical depression. The pain is as heavy as the first day of the loss. It's hard to accept and becomes hard to function in everyday life.

Complicated grief gives you a sense of hopelessness. Feeling sad is normal in loss. However, clinical depression from a loss is grief gone bad. It is that profound sadness that cuts off your lifeline. It can feel like a deep dark pit of suffocation. It denies you the joys of life and can make you feel suicidal.

Your focus is purely internal. Depression robs the griever of their ability to care and show concern for others. Life is about being in community and loving others. Jesus said that we ought to love others as he has loved us. But when our grief has soured, we don't have that desire. We want to withdraw from people. And we welcome the darkness and isolation.

Good grief is the healthy kind. It allows you to interact with others. You will have pockets of laughter and happiness even in the midst of intense pain. It is pain with hope.

Prolonged grief doesn't allow you that privilege. If we find ourselves here, we should seek help from a professional counselor/therapist immediately.

At other times, we can think our grief to be too short. We second-guess ourselves and wonder if we have grieved properly (abbreviated grief) or if we really loved our deceased.

Tears and pain are not the only indicators of love lost. We can love and have joy and peace, even in death. We don't mourn according to the expectations of others. There is nothing to prove to anyone. Our love is our own. No one can see what our hearts feel. So if you cried only once or twice – so, be it. Our sorrow is not timed. A short grief period is neither a good thing or bad. It's just what it is. One person you grieve may take a year, another may take just a few months.

My paternal grandmother and I were very close. I asked her to tell me one desire of her heart. She was 96 years old and I wanted to bless her with a dream of her heart. She replied, gathering her whole family together. I put the plan in motion.

It was a beautiful June afternoon when our family gathered to celebrate our grandmother. Some flew from long distances to be there for the celebration. Granny called me the next morning to say how very pleased and grateful she was. She told me this was it for her. She was now ready to leave the earth. She was satisfied with her celebration and did not want a funeral after she died. Granny died 10 days later. When she passed, I felt her transition. I woke up and knew that she was gone. The phone rang shortly thereafter to relay the news of her passing.

As much as I loved my grandmother, I didn't grieve her in the same way I had grieved others. It seemed only a short time that the severity of the pain lasted. I didn't understand it, at first. But Granny was 4 years shy of 100 and ready for her departure. She had all her affairs in order. And she let it be known, she didn't want to stay here one moment longer. It hurt my heart to lose my grandmother, but my grief was short. Granny had lived a long life. She had a relationship with the Lord, and she was ready. I miss her but I don't shed any more tears and my heart doesn't break when I think of her. I smile and thank God for the honor of having her in my life for so long. I feel especially blessed that my own grandchildren knew her and loved her too.

Good grief is not defined by how long the grief lasts. It is marked by movement towards acceptance of the loss. The pain gradually subsides, and you have the ability to experience life to its fullest.

People will tell you that time heals all wounds. It does take time to get through your loss, however long and short that time is. But time does *not* have the ability to heal all wounds. Jesus does. He is Jehovah-Rapha, our Healer. Hold firmly to his hands as you journey through your grief. Don't cut the time short or prolong it. As they say, a watched pot never boils. That just means we will heal faster if we aren't focused on the speed. Just keep taking those steps forward. There is a wonderful future ahead waiting for you.

Getting to the Good Part:

1. How long have you been grieving your loss?

2. Do you feel it's too long or too short?

3. Have you had any reminders of your pain?

4. Do you wish it was over?

5. What are you doing to heal?

Chapter 10
Strong People Cry

Blessed are they that mourn: for
they shall be comforted. (Matthew 5:4 KJV)

The slogan, "All strength, no sweat" comes from a television ad for a deodorant. Strength and sweat go together when you think about exercise. But the deodorant ad attempts to separate the two. It promotes the idea that you can work hard revealing your strength without any of the inconvenience of sweat. However any trainer worth their weight in gold, will tell you that sweat is a sign of success, when we are working out. Our bodies would overheat if we didn't sweat. Sweating is also good for our immune systems.

Unfortunately we are averse to the body's precipitation. But just as sweat is a sign that we are doing something well, so are tears.

When our eyes sweat, it is a sign that we are doing something well. Our culture tends to misinterpret the lack of tears and strained smiles for strength.

It is unhealthy to instruct someone who is grieving to "be strong" when there is a tragedy or trauma to process. What is meant is "don't cry" or "don't express your grief". The message being relayed is this: in order to be brave or strong, you must stuff your feelings and get on with life. Usually, these unsympathetic words come from someone who doesn't want to feel embarrassed or awkward around those grieving. The guilty party is selfishly looking out for themselves and not those stuck with the loss. Granted, it's hard to be around someone who is crying out of a broken heart and not be touched by their pain. It makes us uncomfortable. Often, we don't have the right words to offer, and we don't know what to do. So, we try to hurry people out of their pain, so we won't have to "be strong".

Real strength is demonstrated when we allow someone to break down in our arms or to sit with them in their silence. Strength is shown when we don't make their grief about us.

Sometimes the message of *tuck in your tears* doesn't come from someone else. Maybe it was the faulty message that was communicated to you as a child. "Don't let them see you sweat."

It's hard because if you aren't permitted to cry when you are in pain, how will you get to your healing?

In our culture, people are encouraged to stuff their emotions and hide their tears especially for men and boys. And so the misconception of what real strength is continues to be propagated.

Real strength is actually the opposite of what our culture tells us. Strong people cry. Crying helps us to release stress and emotional pain. Emotional tears help to release toxins from our bodies. People who aren't allowed to grieve because of societal or familial expectations tend to withdraw emotionally. When they do not know what to do with their grief, they tend to self-medicate with alcohol, drugs, or other destructive substances. Over the long haul, some may become suicidal.

Scientific research has proven that crying releases endorphins (oxytocin and endogenous opioids). These are feel-good hormones. They help to ease both our physical and emotional pain. It is a sure signal of strength when a person expresses grief. He/she is processing their pain. God gave us tears to help us to get to our healthy place.

Psalm 126:5-6 KJV reads, They that sow in tears shall reap in joy.[6] He that goeth forth and weepeth, bearing precious seed, shall doubtless come again with rejoicing, bringing his sheaves with him.

You've kept track of all my wandering and my weeping. You've stored my many tears in your bottle—not one will be lost. For they are all recorded in your book of remembrance. Psalm 56:8 TPT

We are comforted with the promise that our God will redeem our tears. We may go through a dark season but there is a promise of joy on the other side of it. God loves us so much that he will account for every tear that we shed. He, who is rich in mercy, cares about everything that concerns us. Not one tear will be lost on him.

So it is those people who are able to express their grief who will get to the other side of it. They are the strong. But those who contain their tears, refusing to release what is necessary become stagnated in their healing. They are weakened because of it.

When Lazarus died, Jesus wept (John 11:35). Read that again. Jesus wept. There wasn't a single tear slowly strolling down his face. But this scripture indicates there was full fledge weeping. Wept is its past tense. He was expressing deep sorrow by shedding tears and sobbing.

Tears are a necessary part of our process. We need to embrace them. It's the way that God wired us.

Certainly, we do not mourn as those who have no hope. We don't fall apart by jumping into caskets or having a physical temper tantrum. I Thess 4:13-14 AMP. Now we do not want you to be uninformed, believers, about those who are asleep [in death], so that you will not grieve [for them] as the others do who have no hope [beyond this present life]. [14] For if we believe that Jesus died and rose again [as in fact He did], even so God [in this same way—by raising them from the dead] will bring with Him those [believers] who have fallen asleep in Jesus.

We don't act as if we are losing our minds and we can't go on.

We trust that we will get to the other side of sorrow. We will have times when we feel broken and we may try to put on a "brave face" to demonstrate our resilience. But sometimes what we really need is a release. We may need to sit on the bed and let the tears fall, listen to a comforting song and just let go. It's in that moment of vulnerability that we are able to find strength.

God accounts for every salty drop. We can lean on Him. He is the Prince of Peace and the God of all comfort. He wraps His loving arms around us and pulls us close.

Allow yourself the space and time to weep. When someone says be strong, let's normalize that to mean go ahead and have a good cry.

It is in this moment of letting it all out that we find healing, strength, and peace. We can see the gentleness of our Lord. So whether you feel strong or not. The scriptures remind us that the weak should say, "I'm strong." Surely God's strength is made perfect in our weakness.

Getting to the Good Part:

1. Do you believe that crying is a sign of strength? What were you taught growing up?

2. Have you cried since your loved one transitioned?

3. Write down a memory that stands out to you about your loved one.

4. What are some things that trigger your pain?

5. Take a moment to watch a video or view pictures of your loved one.

Chapter 11
Death Trap

And when they say to you, "Seek those who are mediums and wizards, who whisper and mutter," should not a people seek their God? Should they seek the dead on behalf of the living? (Isaiah 8:19 KJV)

"My deceased loved one showed up in my bedroom or my dreams to talk to me." Have you ever heard someone say that? It's dangerous. The enemy sends a smoke screen. It's really not what it appears to be.

People who have a hard time letting go of their loved ones are usually the ones who have such visitations. These visitations are familiar spirits and not the spirits of your loved one. Familiar spirits are assigned by Satan to entice you away from God.

Talking to your loved ones after they have transitioned from this life is a dangerous trap. The only person that we can legitimately communicate with (after death) is Jesus. He was raised to life. We can't pray to any other source.

I Timothy 2:5 puts it this way, For there is one God, and one mediator between God and men, the man Christ Jesus;

Jesus welcomes our conversation. Whatever we want to talk about, He is ready to listen. But we put our loved ones in the place of Christ when we begin to talk to them or pray to them. It is idolatry.

We must be careful not to become attached to the dead. This happens when we have prolonged or complicated grief and refuse to accept that the deceased has transitioned from this life. And so we try to hold on to them through communication with familiar spirits.

It is when we experience loss that we are most susceptible. We are brokenhearted and yearning for the one that has transitioned from this life. And so the enemy is able to entice us if we are open to him. Psychics, sorcerers, mediums, fortune tellers, wizards, séances, etc. all of these workers of divination specialize in death. Their aim is to convince you that they are able to summon your dead loved ones so that you can speak with them.

Those who consult the dead will communicate bits of *accurate* information to string you along until you are given over to the spirit. This idea of talking to the dead is used to bypass God to either discern the past or discover the future to get answers for life. The goal is to get God's information without Him.

Our perspective of death has to be in line with the scriptures. We serve a living God that we have access through Jesus Christ. He has victory over death. So we glory in eternal life that he offers us. We do not glorify death or the dead, it will lead us into idolatry.

God loves people and wants an intimate relationship with all of us. So we have to enter the spirit realm in the correct way, through Jesus Christ. Or else we open ourselves up for demonic influence.

You cannot worship God and your dead family (ancestors). It is sin. You shall have no other gods before me. Exodus 20:3

The Bible refers to ancestral worship as another form of

idolatry. Our ancestors have no control of what is happening in our lives, whether they were believers or not. They can never transcend God's sovereignty.

Good grief allows us to let go of those who are no longer with us. You can keep your memories, but you cannot hold on to the person. Release them from this life. If they know God, you will see them again on the other side.

The Mexican culture celebrates the day of the dead. It is a Mexican holiday where families welcome back the souls of their deceased relatives for a reunion that includes food, drink and celebration. According to their tradition, the gates of heaven are opened and the spirits of children can rejoin their families for 24 hours. And the following day, the spirits of adults can do the same. African celebrations also celebrate during this time period. The families decorate the graves with offerings to attract the souls of the dead.

These are demon spirits sent by Satan to seduce those who are open to them. Even Christians have been found to be involved with these anti-Christian acts. Cultural rituals do not supersede the word of God.

The enemy is able to take us captive when we are reluctant to let go of our loved ones when they die. But understand this - your family members cannot come back to the earth at will. Nor can they be summoned back. Once they have exited this earth, they won't return. It is the act of witches and warlocks to summon demon spirits and celebrate death, dying and the dead.

As believers, we live by every Word of God. It's how we measure all things. What is God's heart on the subject? We must always agree with Him, regardless of our cultural traditions.

Our society has shifted over the last 20 years. Sadly, standards are established by what is popular.

Today, when a loved one dies, lavish parties are thrown, and some are even held in the cemetery or as they are walking to/from the cemetery with big bands almost like a Mardi Gras event. Many are moving away from the traditional church services and throwing a type of wild celebration instead. Unfortunately there is no one speaking to the bereaved about their own mortality. There is no one encouraging the people to make sure they see Christ in peace. We are erasing God's voice from this sensitive time in people's lives. One train of thought is- it's too uncomfortable to talk about where we will go when we leave the earth. So let's throw a party instead.

Some even make life-size pictures and cutouts of the deceased to sort of memorialize them. It's their way of keeping the deceased alive. And if they have a cutout in their home, it's hard to discard. Nine times out of ten, they will talk to that cutout. Some even say that it talks back to them.

Another new thing in connection with the dead is birthday and anniversary parties that are held for the dead. A birthday is a celebration of another year of life. So how does one host a birthday party for someone who has died? That person is not another year older. Birthdays and anniversaries stop when we die. We have to accept that. We can't continue to count the days when the days have ended.

The earth is no longer relevant to those who have transitioned. Believers will live forever. So we don't number our days in heaven like we do on the earth.

If you want to remember your loved one on their birthdate, you can. Do it in a way that honors God. Give to their church, ministry, or other charity. Help a senior citizen, child, or the poor. But be careful of falling into idolatrous acts.

Avoid Other Dark Activity like

- Shrines in honor of the dead
- Seances
- Ouija boards
- Talking to grave
- Holding onto the ashes of the deceased

We have to ask ourselves, why are we participating in this activity? Why do we save ashes? What's the purpose? Is this act giving God glory?

Angels Watching Over Us

Another mistaken belief is the notion that our loved ones die and become angels. Scripture does not support this. Dead humans do not become angels. God created everything after its own kind. A human does not morph into an angel upon death. A human is still a human. Their spirit returns to the Lord. They are not privy to the comings and goings of earth. Nor could a mere human handle the enormous task of watching over us. That is a God-sized job. He alone is omniscient – (all knowing) and omnipresent (He can see everything at all times) and omnipotent (all powerful). And so He enlists his ministering angels and gives them charge over us.

We do not conjure up the dead or talk to the dead. It is ungodly. No dead person can make things happen for us.

Leviticus 19:31 'Give no regard to mediums and familiar spirits; do not seek after them, to be defiled by them: I *am* the LORD your God.'

We have to decide who we will trust – spirits masking as our dead loved ones or Our Gracious Daddy God.

We can't immortalize those who have preceded us. It's a pretense. They cannot physically or even spiritually live on in the earth. It's a scheme of the enemy to try to bypass the way to eternal life. The only way to live forever is through Jesus Christ. There is no other way.

The Bible says that man's days are fleeting. We will not live on this earth forever.

Psalm 103:15-16 KJV *As for* man, his days *are* as grass: as a flower of the field, so he flourisheth. For the wind passeth over it, and it is gone; and the place thereof shall know it no more.

None of us came to the earth to stay. When we exit the earth, it is all over. And it's only what we have done for Christ that will matter in the end. There is no bringing us back or talking to us after it's done. As much as we love our family and friends, we cannot get caught up in this death trap. We must love and honor God more than people. He is the One who gifted to us those we love so much.

Getting to the Good Part:

1. Have you participated in inappropriate rituals for your loved one?

2. In what way can you honor your loved one without dishonoring God?

3. What was your loved one's strengths?

4. What do you want to remember most about them?

Chapter 12
What Becomes of the Broken Hearted?

The LORD is near to the brokenhearted and saves the crushed in spirit. (Psalm 34:18 KJV)

Sadness is a normal and appropriate response to loss. We have to allow it to run its course without letting it morph into full blown depression, which affects our overall quality of life. Over time, the intensity of the pain of your loss will subside. Things will <u>never</u> return to normal. So don't expect normal. But you will adjust your life to accommodate the loss. You will learn how to live without the physical presence of the decedent. I know you won't want to, but it is necessary to finish your assignment. We don't get to quit living because someone we loved died. We have more time than they had. Baking a cake takes longer than baking biscuits. But I don't throw away my cake because the biscuits are done. The cake must continue to bake.

It hurts to continue without our loved ones. However we cannot allow ourselves to be swallowed up in the quicksand of depression.

When your heart is broken, you have to take time to let it heal properly. That means you will need to trust God through the process. The scripture in Isaiah 53:3 tells us that Jesus was a man of sorrows acquainted with grief. He wants us to get it that He understands. He volunteered for His sorrows. He was intimate with grief because of His steadfast love for us.

He is near to the brokenhearted (Psalm 34:18). So close your eyes and imagine that the Lord is close to you, right in the middle of your pain. When you move, he does too. When all the mourners go to their homes, he remains close to you. He is not turned off by your pain or trying to rush you out of it.

Our kind and compassionate King is there to offer you peace and comfort and to help you put your loss into perspective.

Although there are times that you may feel alone, you are not. The Lord refuses to allow his people to walk though grief without him.

While your heart is mending, God asks that you let Him in. Don't hold your pain too tightly to your chest, as if it's all you have left of your loved one. Trust Him. He wants to sit with you in your pain. You can't make sense of it outside of him.

Sometimes he sits with us in our stillness and other times he speaks a few words at a time. Maybe you will hear just one scripture verse or a single word. But whatever he says, it is enough. Journal through your journey. Write down the words that he gives. They will help your perspective and bring you hope, and healing.

Though others may not understand the depth of your loss, God does. And he will stand with you. After everyone has gone back to their regular lives, know that God remains.

For we do not have a High Priest who is unable to sympathize and understand our weaknesses and temptations, but One who has been tempted [knowing exactly how it feels to be human] in every respect as we are, yet without [committing any] sin.

Hebrews 4:14 AMP

When you bring your pain to him, He promises to give you a spiritual exchange in Isaiah 61:3.

The writer says that the Lord will grant us beauty for our ashes, gladness for our mourning, praise for our heaviness and peace for our hopelessness.

We give him all the negative that we are experiencing, and he gives us the better gifts. What a great swap. Give him all the loss, hurt, and anger, and bitterness. He will swap it out and grant to us beauty, gladness, praise, and peace.

I want that. You want it, too. But you have to be open to it. We serve an incredible God. His lovingkindness is better than life. He is always looking for ways to bless his people. I don't know why anyone wouldn't want to serve Him. The same God who takes the punishment for our sin is always asking for us to give him our burdens.

I Peter 5:7 AMP reads, casting all your cares [all your anxieties, all your worries, and all your concerns, once and for all] on Him, for He cares about you [with deepest affection, and watches over you very carefully].

Matthew 11:28-30 KJV Come unto me, all ye that labour and are heavy laden, and I will give you rest.

²⁹ Take my yoke upon you, and learn of me; for I am meek and lowly in heart: and ye shall find rest unto your souls.

³⁰ For my yoke is easy, and my burden is light.

When we are weary, we are to cast our cares on the Lord. Another exchange. Give him all the ugly and he gives us the beauty. Give him the heavy and he gives us the light.

Psalm 30:5 AMP For His anger is but for a moment, His favor is for a lifetime. Weeping may endure for a night, but a shout of joy comes in the morning.

What an amazing promise! God favors his people with joy. You may weep now, but joy is on the way. The sun will shine again. Our hearts will know laughter and love again. A new day is coming. We may be brokenhearted right now, but it is not a life sentence. We will overcome. All things broken will be restored.

Joy is a gift. We have to learn how to invite it into our hearts, especially in the midst of loss. Accept it when it comes. Don't refuse it. It's really okay to smile or laugh in your season of grief. Thank God for those moments. The more you receive those joy moments, the more they will increase. Look for joy. Expect it. Know that no matter what season you are in, there is a place for joy. And it's joy that helps you get to good grief.

We have a promise that when we get to the other side God will have done away with death, grief, and loss. Revelation 21:4 And God will wipe away every tear from their eyes; there shall be no more death, nor sorrow, nor crying. There shall be no more pain, for the former things have passed away."

Grief is only on this side. We won't know it in the next realm. But we can get through it when we trust in Jesus. We will feel the ugly pain of loss and death, but we will never go through it alone. God promises to be right there with us to help us through it. Take him up on His Word. Hear Him, dear one. Your assignment is not complete. You can't stop here. Access your promises by faith. There is still so much more life to live. Journey through good grief. Purpose awaits.

Getting to the Good Part:

1. Spend time in prayer. Record what you believe God is

saying to you about what you should do next.

2. Respond back to Him.

3. What are you doing to get to the good part of your grief?

4. What is the hardest part of your journey?

5. What good have you discovered in this season?

Scriptures for Comfort

2 Corinthians 1:3-4 KJV Blessed be God, even the Father of our Lord Jesus Christ, the Father of mercies, and the God of all comfort; ⁴ Who comforteth us in all our tribulation, that we may be able to comfort them which are in any trouble, by the comfort wherewith we ourselves are comforted of God.

Jeremiah 31:13b KJV for I will turn their mourning into joy. And will comfort them and make them rejoice from their sorrow.

Psalm 116:15 KJV Precious in the sight of the Lord is the death of His saints.

Isaiah 25:8 AMP He will swallow up death [and abolish it] for all time. And the Lord GOD will wipe away tears from all faces, And He will take away the disgrace of His people from all the earth; For the LORD has spoken.

Matthew 5:4 KJV Blessed are they that mourn: for they shall be comforted.

II Corinthians 5:8 AMP We are [as I was saying] of good courage and confident hope, and prefer rather to be absent from the body and to be at home with the Lord.

Revelation 21:4 KJV And God will wipe away every tear from their eyes; there shall be no more death, nor sorrow, nor crying. There shall be no more pain, for the former things have passed away."

John 14:1-3 TPT "Don't worry or surrender to your fear. For you've believed in God, now trust and believe in me also. ² My Father's house has many dwelling places. If it were otherwise, I would tell you plainly, because I go to prepare a place for you. ³ And when everything is ready, I will come back and take you to myself so that you will be where I am.

Romans 8:28 KJV And we know that all things work together for good to them that love God, to them who are the called according to his purpose.

I Peter 5:7 AMP Casting all your cares [all your anxieties, all your worries, and all your concerns, once and for all] on Him, for He cares about you [with deepest affection, and watches over you very carefully].

Deuteronomy 31:6 AMP Be strong and courageous, do not be afraid or tremble in dread before them, for it is the LORD your God who goes with you. He will not fail you or abandon you.

John 16:22 KJV And ye now therefore have sorrow: but I will see you again, and your heart shall rejoice, and your joy no man taketh from you.

About the Author

Crystal Jones is a publisher, author, mentor, and speaker. She celebrates nearly 40 years of marriage with her husband and best friend, Oscar Jones. She has 5 children, 3 bonus children-in-law, and 11 grandchildren. The couple has planted two churches and cover 12 other ministries. They have a dynamic marriage ministry, Marriage for a Lifetime Ministries (Detroit, MI). Crystal also leads the Fearless Women's Movement, hosting conferences across the country.

www.ingramcontent.com/pod-product-compliance
Lightning Source LLC
Chambersburg PA
CBHW070855050426
42453CB00012B/2207